Local Marketing For A Small Business

Attract, Create, Retain Customers and Increase Revenue

KRISHNA DIAMESSO

For permissions contact: info@provenmarketingmachine.com

Disclaimer

The information contained within this eBook is strictly for educational purposes. If you wish to apply the ideas contained in this eBook, you are taking full responsibility for your actions.

The author has made every effort to ensure the accuracy of the information within this book was correct at time of publication. The author does not assume and hereby disclaims any liability to any party for any loss, damage, or disruption caused by errors or omissions, whether such errors or omissions result from accident, negligence, or any other cause.

TABLE OF CONTENTS

Table of Contents 4

1 Introduction   8

2 Attract More Customers 12

    2.1 Who is Your Target Market? 12

    2.2 Solve your Customer Problem   16

    2.3 Features and Benefits   17

    2.4 What is Different About Your Business?   17

    2.5 How To Get More Leads?   20

    2.6 Design a Free Information Product   22

    2.7 What Media Should I Use to Reach My Customers?   25

        Business Card   27

        3-Step Letter Advertising 29

        Postcard   30

        Facebook   32

    2.8 Landing Pages 35

3 Retain Customers and Increase Revenue   38

    3.1 Lower the Barrier   39

    3.2 Nurture Leads & Newsletter 41

    3.3 Going Online   44

    Traffic with Blogs 45

    Traffic with Ads   45

        WordPress 46

Landing Page   47

Social Media   48

3.4 Make Use of Google Maps   50

3.5 Huddle   52

3.6 Incentives for Employees.   53

3.7 Educate Your Staff 54

3.8 Develop an Array of Media for Your Business 54

3.9 Market your business with Workshops   57

3.10 Community Events   60

3.11 Customer Thank You Event 62

3.12 Have Contests 63

3.13 Price Strategy 64

3.14 Plugging Leaks   64

3.15 Mailchimp   65

3.16 Customer Relationship Management Software (CRM) 66

3.17 Follow Up Sequence   67

3.18 Partnerships   68

3.19 Tracking 70

3.20 Paid Advertising Effectiveness   70

3.21 Have Fun with Your Marketing 72

3.22 Smile   72

3.23 Your Marketing Schedule   73

3.24 Business is a Collection of Customers   74

3.25 Getting a New Customer is Like Dating 75

3.26 Testimonials   76

3.27 Answer Calls Promptly 77

3.28 Referrals 78

3.29 Continuous Learning   79

4 Outro 80

About the author 84

1 INTRODUCTION

Hello, my name is Krishna.

I have spent countless years looking for the keys to attracting new customers.

I have spent years in different businesses searching for the secret to attracting customers. Many times, I was frustrated with the various techniques taught by so-called gurus that just ended up costing me a fortune.

Until one day, after a business conference, I sat down with a successful man during dinner. I would like to call him a mentor, but I only had the chance of that one dinner with him. He was waiting for his flight which was in a few hours and decided to spare some time with me.

As I was talking to him, asking questions about what he was doing that was working in his business, he laid down his methods and secrets to attracting customers. I barely caught everything, but I did the best I could.

Excited to try it, I put it in action the very next day. And, surprisingly, I received a phone call. Then another. Then another. An abundance of leads. I was able to rework the system with time, and adapt it to different media. I decided that other small business owners should have access to these secrets so they can be successful.

My passion is helping small businesses thrive by helping them solve one of the biggest challenges in business which is to attract leads and turn them into raving customers.

My goal - and the goal of this book - is to help you attract more leads that will make the cash register ring, help you retain more customers and overall make you feel proud of the business you are building. I want to have the small business owner enjoy his business again. Let's face it: business is much more fun when the cash register rings "MONEY."

I am confident that what you are going to learn is going to help you with your goals, if you take the time to apply it.

APPLY. This is the keyword. Often we like reading, but we do not spend enough time in implementation mode or as I like to call it "HUSTLE MODE." You will see the most significant benefit when you can apply the greatest amount of strategies working all in synergy.

But again, all this might be new to you, and you might need some help. That is why I work with a select number of small business owners and offer consulting services.

If you like to know more head to https:// www.provenmarketingmachine.com/free-strategy-session/ or send me an email at consulting@provenmarketingmachine.com.

With that said, we are here to learn how to attract more customers, retain those customers, add more money to the cash register and much more.

One Last Thing.

The word "customers" can easily be switched with "patients", "clients", "members", etc. We will think of a customer, in broad terms, as someone exchanging money for something you offer.

Also, the word "product" can easily be switched with the word "service" and vice versa.

More importantly, think about ways the ideas discussed below can be applied in your business. A small tweak can make all the difference.

Now, let's really get started.

2 ATTRACT MORE CUSTOMERS

2.1 WHO IS YOUR TARGET MARKET?

When you look at the word "marketing," there is a strong emphasis on the word "market." This should force you to understand that without a market or better yet a target market you cannot have marketing.

Any group of people can be a market but is it the right market for you? That is why we need to zero in and look at your target market. You need to know who your customer is.

When I say "who is your customer?", you probably have in your business right now someone you consider as your best customer.

Look at your customer base. Who are your best clients, who

spend the most, who visit your store often, in which industry are they, what do they like, who refers you client, what is their age, their city, their gender, who responds to your emails or phone calls the most, what common denominator do you observe? Once you're able to look at that information and analyze it, I'm sure you're going to come up with a type of person that you feel you resonate the most with and they resonate the most with you.

Think about that person and try to imagine him. Sometimes it's not only one person. What we're talking about here are the characteristics that are familiar and common among a few people that do business with you.

If you're not in business right now, you have to think about who will fit the most with what you're selling.

Why should you zero in on your customer? Well, because it is less expensive to market to that segment. If you try to go too broad, you will spend a lot more money. It's not efficient. As a small business, you need to be focused. With a narrow market, you're able to develop products and services that are an exact match for them. Your marketing is more potent and powerful.

Once you define who that customer is, you're going to find that it's a lot easier to figure out where your customers hang out, what do those customers read, where do they go online. Finding them is a lot easier.

Let's say, for example, our customer is a 25 to 35 year old man who likes video games, works at a finance corporation, drives a Honda sedan and has a kid or two. You know that your customer likes games and is in finance. It's a lot easier now to know some of the things that they're going to be attracted to or that they do on a regular basis. Maybe they're into magazines that talk about games, maybe they watch a lot of YouTube or TV shows that review games, or everything that is game related. Your business does not need to be related to games to advertise in a game magazine. You know where your customer is, and you can target them.

You also want to focus on one market to avoid message dissonance. This is when your marketing message does not match your market.

If you focus on everybody with your advertising, some people are going to resonate with it, and some other people are not. But if you're able to zero in on a specific target market, you know their demographics, you know what they respond to, everything is about them, everything is talking to them, then you'll have a much better response.

Advertising for a single woman in Ohio with a kid and advertising for a young adult male working in finance in New York City are two different things. We have two different personas; they're not attracted to the same thing.

To establish a target market for consumers, you look at age, city, demography, income, etc. For business, it tends to be a little different, but not too much. If you're business-to-business, you can target the years the company has been in operation, the number of employees, their revenues, etc. All that information is going to give you a target market that you can go after.

You need to keep this in mind when choosing a target market.

Do not take this lightly. Knowing your target market is the very first thing in marketing that you should do. Take the time to draw a profile of your customer.

2.2 SOLVE YOUR CUSTOMER PROBLEM

The next thing we're going to look at is the problem that we are trying to solve for our customer. What is their main problem right now? Are they trying to lose weight, are they trying to make more money? We need to define what their problem is.

With that problem comes a few challenges that they might have.

Let's take an example here of somebody who has back pain. Their main problem is back pain. With that back pain, it also means that they can no longer practice sports regularly, or they can no longer walk for a long distance without strain.

Those are some of the challenges that the customer is having. When you know them, and you can define them, your customers are going to relate to you because you understand them.
The solution that your services or products offer should be the answer to the main problem and/or the challenges that the customer has.

2.3 FEATURES AND BENEFITS

Now let's look at what you should do when describing your solution. A lot of people mostly focus on the features. They don't focus enough on the benefits. What does the customer get with the features?

A common example is when we look at a vehicle. The vehicle has airbags. The feature is going to be: "12 360-degree airbags inside the car", but the benefit to the customer is that the customer will be protected from all sides in case of an accident. This will reduce the chance of them being severely injured or losing their life. That is the benefit to the customer, and you need to look at what each feature is doing for the customers.

One thing you can do is look at each feature of your product or service and try to add at the end: "This benefits you in" or "Is a benefit to you." In the example of the airbag, you can say that the 360-degree airbag "benefits you in" case of an accident you will be safe.

2.4 WHAT IS DIFFERENT ABOUT YOUR BUSINESS?

What is different and better about your business? In your field, there is a lot of competition. There is competition everywhere, in every field. If you are in an industry that doesn't have competition you either have found gold or you are in a risky or low potential business/industry. Probably, other people have found out that it is not lucrative. But you could well-be a trailblazer.

For any business right now there is always competition, but the best thing you can do is try to differentiate yourself. How can you differentiate yourself?

Let's look at a few examples of businesses that differentiate themselves through positioning of time. We can look at a restaurant in town where you won't wait to be seated, or we can look at a dentist in town where appointments are guaranteed to last only 30-45 minutes. For customers that value time, this is very powerful because they know that they can allocate those 30 minutes and be on their way.

There are different ways you can differentiate yourself. Some people call it having a unique selling proposition or USP or positioning your business, but it's really about what makes you different.

If I mention FedEx, you will know the company represents speed of delivery.

If I mention Louis Vuitton, you know it is luxury.

Another illustration that I can give you is when you look at computers, you have Windows, and you have Macs. Windows is an operating system that everybody can get that is not too expensive. You can do your office work for a relatively low amount of money. Macs are more about great designs, finesse, creativity. People also know that you're not going to find Macs at the same price that you will find a Windows computer, it's far more expensive.

People know that if I'm creative, I'll go for a Mac. But if I'm more in administration or office work, I'll go for a Windows computer.

Try to find a way where you can differentiate your business, find a quality that you could focus on and when people think of you they will think about that quality as well.

A good way that you can find what makes you different is to ask your very best customers why are they buying from you. You'll be surprised about some of the answers that you will hear. They might be buying from you because they saw something in you that you don't even realize.

Asking your best customer why they buy from you will definitely help you find a way to decide to focus on one thing. That's going to be your positioning, that's going to be your unique selling proposition. That's where you're strong, that is where you differentiate yourself from what your competition is doing.

You need to differentiate yourself. When people will think of you, what would come to mind? Are you going to differentiate yourself through speed, through a new creative process, through the number of services offered?

2.5 HOW TO GET MORE LEADS?

You need to have a system that lets customers get to know you.

One of the main mistakes that businesses do for their marketing is advertising their name, logo, some features about their business and a phone number requesting the customer to call.

The customer doesn't yet know you and is not incentivized to call you.

It is a mistake to do that. The best thing that you can do to multiply and increase the leads that you get is through a lead generation system.

A lead generation system? What is it? I am glad you asked.

A lead generation system works when, instead of asking the customer to call you at your place of business to buy your products or services, you're offering information to the customer to capture their contact information.

We're in the information age. Information drives our economy.

When you look at Google, Facebook, YouTube, social media and a lot of the other things out there, you will notice that information is at the center of what they provide. People are looking for information. People have problems, and people are looking for solutions to those problems.

Most of the time, when people go on Google, they look for "how to": "how to solve my problem," "how to ease my back pain," "how to save money," "how to invest." When you focus on this and provide a solution to those how-tos, you will thrive.

2.6 DESIGN A FREE INFORMATION PRODUCT

Part of what is needed for your lead generation system is designing a free information product.

In what format can you give away your free information product? You can give away a CD, a DVD, a PDF, or a book.

It is also a lot more potent when you're able to combine all of those into one kit package. It could be a package where you're going to have a CD and a DVD and a book altogether, and you are going to send that to your customer. Nobody (maybe 1% only) is doing that in your industry right now. This is going to push you to differentiate yourself from your competitors.

But watch your cost. Make sure it all makes sense financially.

You're going to offer the report to your leads through all your marketing. Your lead generation marketing should present something for free, which is easy to do with information. The primary objective of the information will be to offer a solution to one of the challenges or main problem that your ideal customer is having.

When you advertise, you should have instructions that your customer is going to follow that will drive him to a landing page or an 800 number.

The principles are the same for the landing page and a free 800 number. The customer should leave his/her information. On the 800 number, you will have a recording playing and telling the customer about your free report available and what they need to do to request it.

On the landing page, you're going to have the information about the free product that you're trying to give away as well.

You will present very briefly the solution that you're providing in the report. The customer is going to enter their name and email address to get that report.

This is where the relationship starts.

You are getting a lead by getting the name and email of the customer. The customer is getting a report from you that's supposed to have part of the solution to the problems that they have.

An information "product" could also be a free workshop or a free consultation, depending on your business. But usually, the farther remove you are from the information product, the easier it will be to get the contact information of the customer. They will not think that you will try to sell them.

One thing I need to emphasize before continuing is as an entrepreneur or business owner you need to focus on solving the problem of customers. People have problems and challenges in their life, and if you can solve their problems, they are going to be giving you money for that.

We have discussed how to get the information from a customer. The customer information should go into a database. This kind of database is often called a Customer Relationship Management software (CRM).

The CRM is going to have the list of all the leads that have requested your report. It will have the name, email, and address (and some other extra information) of your leads but would also store your current customers.

Depending on the CRM, it could also have the different actions that a customer actually took in their journey within your marketing. As an example, it will highlight that the customer downloaded your report, and later on went to a new page when you sent them an email. It will also highlight that the customer clicked on the email that you sent them. It is a centralized database that gives you a lot of information about the different actions your leads or customers are taking.

2.7 WHAT MEDIA SHOULD I USE TO REACH MY CUSTOMERS?

You have a lot of options here. You could reach your customers through a magazine, TV, Radio, newspapers…. but we are looking for something that's not going to take a lot of time at first, that we can start with ease and is also flexible on the budget. We can start small, but we can scale and increase it as well if we want.

When deciding on a medium one of the main things to look at is the target market that you're trying to go for. Reaching a 70 year old man on Facebook might not be the best way to go. They do not hang out there.

Some media might work a little bit better than others depending on the market. That is why it's vital to first test and look at your results.

The media that we're going to look at are business cards, postcards, a 3 step-letter, and Facebook/Google.

We want to be able to advertise offline and online. You are covering all the bases. Some customers do not spend a lot of time online. To get to them, an offline outreach will be the way to go.

In the same fashion, other customers might tune out offline media. For them, an outreach online might work better.

Not relying on one single method is the best strategy you could have. Things change and a source of business that was working yesterday might no longer work tomorrow.

Business Card

On the business card, you will modify your information slightly. You're going to have information that you have currently: your name, place of business, business name. On the back, you're going to have a headline. It's going to be a question or statement that refers to the customer's problem, plus a call to action driving to a landing page (or phone number, or workshop).

Example:

Front

Dr. Charles Philip

Chiropractor

50 Lincoln Street, Brooklyn, NY 1125

Back

Free Report Reveals How to Ease Your Lower Back Pain Fast With 7 Easy Exercises

Go to www.7easyexercices.com to download your Free Report.

We're coming back to the free report that we talked about earlier. To reiterate, your lead generation advertising will drive back to that landing page and the free report so the customer can leave their name and email address.

We want to do that because it allows us to market later on again to our would-be customer, to follow up with the customer, to nurture the customer, because all our leads are not ready to buy right now.

It has been said that only 3%-10% of customers who see your advertising are ready to buy at the moment. You will be losing 90% of customers if you do not capture information from those customers and follow up with them. You are throwing money away.

It's imperative that at first, you capture the name, email address, and address if you can.

You can also offer the report as a backup. What I mean is that you can lead with your main product for sale but you can also specify that for those that are not ready to buy now there is a report, workshop or consultation available. At the end, when the customer shows up for the workshop and consultation, you are still able to collect their contact information for future marketing.

If you have a physical store, a way to adapt it would be to offer a gift or a certain promotion to the customer. They would leave their business card, and you could market to them later on.

On the phone as well, your goal should be to get the contact information of your customers and right away send an information package.

3-Step Letter Advertising

Another strategy for offline advertising is to use a 3-step letter campaign. What we often associate with a letter in an envelope is usually something that could be important. It could be something coming from a friend or the government. We pay more attention to it.

With a 3-step letter, you will have your first letter reaching out to the customer and explaining your offer. If you don't hear back from that customer, you will send your second letter. If the customer still does not respond to your second letter, you will close with a third letter. The third letter will somehow mention that you sorry you haven't heard back from them but that your door is still open.

Letters cost a little more than postcards, but you also have more real estate and are therefore able to give more details about what you offer.

Postcard

The postcard will be about the same as our business card. Where it will change is now we have more real estate; we can have on the postcard a lot more information. We can probably add features and benefits.

Example:

Free Report Reveals How to Ease Your Lower Back Pain Fast With 7 Easy Exercises

Go to www.7easyexercices.com to download your Free Report.

The exercises that you will learn in the report will help you:

- Sleep more deeply at night

- Increase your breathing

- Play tennis again

- Relax your joints

- Best of all, you can do them in 5 minutes, and they don't require an exercise mat!

Advertise the solution to their problem and craft a headline and the benefits for your target market.

Once you have your postcard ready, you will need to distribute it. Your post office will be your ally. In Canada and the USA, the post office has a program that allows you to target consumers and businesses within a specific mail route or radius of a zip code or address. You can reach out to your post office to learn more.

But also, the post office works with partner businesses whose only job is to help you get your marketing out. You won't need to figure out as many details by yourself if you decide to go with one of the partners, and you can stay focused on your business. Reach out to them as well, get a quote, and send your new postcard to a small test number of targets and expand as you go. Make the post office work for you.

Facebook

For Facebook, you will need a picture and a headline. If you already did your business card and your postcard or already thought about it, it's going to be about the same. You will drive the customer to a landing page to get more information and download a free report there. You're going to highlight what the customers are going to get in your advertising.

One of the reasons why we go on Facebook is because it allows us to zero in on a particular target market.

You can use other places to advertise, but Facebook is user-friendly.

You could also use Google Adwords. Google Adwords and Facebook can be quite similar, though Adwords has an emphasis on keywords. On Facebook, you're able to go in and set the target market that we discussed before and to advertise only to those people. You can focus on people who like sports, people who like a certain celebrity, people who like a specific Facebook page.

Choosing between Facebook and Google Adwords will depend on your type of business, what you want to achieve and the type of promotion you run.

When customers are looking for a certain business or professional, they first turn to Google.

Lifestyle businesses such as gyms, restaurants, retail clothing store are great for Facebook because you can easily share photos and videos.

At the end of the day, you want to be omnipresent. You want to show up everywhere as long as your budget allows it.

Facebook can be quite ninja. You have the possibility of doing some retargeting or setting up custom audiences. You can also have video ads which take your message to a whole new level. But start small, get an ad up and running quickly and learn more about the Facebook Ad platform. You will eventually be able to do more advanced advertising.

Facebook can be flexible for a lot of businesses, but it depends if you can reach your target market through that medium. That is why having different media through which you can advertise is essential.

The postcard, business card, and Facebook are reasonably easy to start with. You already have your business card. A postcard is easy to send out. It's about a dollar or 2 dollars per postcard with shipping, printing, everything included. And you can be up and running on Facebook for about 10-20 dollars a day.

The 3-step letter would require a little more effort. But it is affordable and scalable.

What is recommended, though, is the more media you can

advertise with, the better it is. You're not going to depend on any one medium. If you only depend on one medium, it's really dangerous. If there's a change in regulation, price, or your customer moving away from that medium, you can be in trouble.

It's best to diversify with several media. The more you have, the better.

If you want to be stable, start with those three, but increase to four or five as soon as you can. The analogy here is just like when you're driving a car you have four tires. You actually have five tires with the spare. If one of your media doesn't perform as well as you want to, you can easily switch it.

But the most ideal position would be to do as much as your budget allows. You can diversify with radio, TV, YouTube, etc. anywhere you can be. Once you're able to fine-tune your advertising, your landing page, and all those elements we have seen here you can be whenever and wherever you want to be.

2.8 LANDING PAGES

Most of your advertising should be driven to a dedicated landing page where possible. When you advertise a free workshop, you might not need a landing page. You could, depending on your situation, ask the customer to give you a call to register. On the call, you will capture the necessary contact information of your customers.

Landing pages are very powerful.

When you advertise, everything that doesn't match what was advertised will reduce your conversion rate.

A lot of companies make this mistake. They will have their advertising with their name, business name, phone number, and their website. They will also send traffic to their main website. This is throwing leads and money away.

With a landing page, you're able to increase your conversion rate because you have one message and that was the one message you discussed in the advertisement that the customer saw.

It's a better user experience for the customer because it's giving them exactly what they are looking for. There's only one intent, and the customer can take a single action based on the intent. And you can capture their name, email and maybe their address as well.

3 RETAIN CUSTOMERS AND INCREASE REVENUE

Earlier we looked at different ways to attract new leads, but the truth is attracting new leads all the time is very expensive. What you need to focus on is finding ways to retain your customers and attend to their needs.

If you have been in business for a number of years, you have acres of diamonds in your backyard. You should find ways to leverage your current assets and customers to bring your business to new heights.

The following strategies will help in retaining your customers and putting more money in your business.

3.1 LOWER THE BARRIER

You need to find a way to lower the barrier, lower the obstacles or the resistance that your customer might have before buying your product or service.

You have a few options to lower the barrier for customers to try your services or products. You could have a free consultation, a free audit, a free sample box that you can send to customers, a free education seminar, a free trial, or a free report. Give your customers a way to test your products or services without losing anything or losing too much. Once they know what you are about, they will be more inclined to get the full product if it helps them solve their problems.

Brainstorm ways that customers, leads, and prospects could try your services and products without a lot of cost on their end. Here is a short story. I was working with a Toastmaster group that had a serious problem with getting new members.

They had the usual "come to try us and become a member" offer. I quickly figured out that one session wasn't enough for them to get a feel for what they were about to sign up for. My team and I decided to move it to 3 free sessions, which no other group was doing. We were not losing much by moving to a 3-session trial: the room was already paid off with the help of the current members. We changed a few other things as well. Even though guests were just visiting and it was their first meeting, we tried to get them involved right away so they would know what it would be like going forward. In a short amount of time, we tripled the membership and had a waiting list.

Guests were able to see what the club was really about. They were already making friends with other members, so it was harder for them to abandon it because they already felt like they were members.

Brainstorm ways where you could do the same in your business or let people experience your product for a longer time.

You also have the example of the puppy close. You might have heard of it. With the pressure of a family member, usually kids, you go to see some puppies. The kids want a puppy, you not that much. At the store, they tell you to get the puppy for the night or the weekend, and if the puppy isn't to your liking, you could easily return it.

They don't charge you anything. A lot of times, you end up keeping the puppy. You say to yourself: "This puppy doesn't seem too bad, I guess we can keep him."

Another example is a test drive at a car dealership. Instead of the 5-minute test drive around the block, they're probably going to recommend that the salesman goes for a 30-minute drive. Why? The more you find yourself driving the car, the more you would want to purchase it.

Find ways where people can experience your product for a longer period. The more they experience it, and the earlier they experience it, the better.

3.2 NURTURE LEADS & NEWSLETTER

If you don't already have a newsletter, that should be the first thing that you should put in place because it's just that important.

I have mentioned before that not everybody is ready to buy right now. Once a lead gives you their name and email, they get into your database and automatically you should have a sequence of emails that goes out to the customer.

The reason for that is the customer gets to know you a little bit; they get to see what you're up to, what you're about, they discover you. Before seeing your advertising, the customer didn't know about you. You were a stranger.

The newsletter is going to let the customer get to know you. This will be part of your email marketing strategy where you will combine promoting your services and/or products and educating the customer.

Regarding education and selling, you need to have a balance. You could have a 75% focus with your emails on education and 25% focus on selling. Focus on education because the customer will see the value in staying on your list. Create a balance because if you are always trying to sell your customers, nobody likes that and they will unsubscribe, and you have lost a customer for good.

Some other things you can mention in your email will be things that happen in your business, results that a customer or clients recently had, things that happened in your life as well, customers surveys, and accomplishments. They will get to know you, get to trust you and end up buying from you.

If you implement a newsletter, I am pretty sure that you will see real benefits within a few months.

A newsletter also helps remind your customers that you exist. There is a lot of competition out there, and if you are not proactively in front of your customers, they will forget you.

We all do that sometimes. Life happens, things happen. You meant to do something, or you were getting products or services from a specific business, but life got in a way. When you send your newsletter, then you're able to remind the people that stopped doing business with you that you exist. They might have meant to come to your place of business again, but they just forgot because life got in a way.

A tax specialist would only see most of his clients once every year with very few interactions in between. With a newsletter, every month, their customers would get tips on how to prepare for the next tax season, how to have a better return, free tips that the tax specialist would share. When it would come time for tax season again, those customers would think of him. The tax specialist is proactive in getting business.

Without being strategic about marketing and retaining customers, the tax specialist might think that all the people they did business with last year will return the next year. There is a chance that he is not tracking that information and he doesn't know if it's the case or not. A customer could slip away and go to another tax specialist and the tax specialist would not know.

Newsletters are really powerful. If you don't do the other things I'm talking about here, you should implement a newsletter, and you will notice a major change in your business.

3.3 GOING ONLINE

You probably know that nowadays having a website is important. The most important feature of your website is your blog.

In your blog, you can display your expertise.

Traffic with Blogs

Once you have a blog, you have different ways to get traffic. You have paid traffic and organic traffic. You get organic traffic the more you post. The more your information gets spread out on the web and search engines can find it, the more traffic you will get.

Search engines can index your website because they like when regular updates are done on a website. For search engines, it means the website is active. With search engines indexing more of your site, your leads and customers can find you easily.

In addition to writing posts on your website; you can also guest blog. With guest blogging, you write blogs on other websites that you partner with. Those guest posts will later link to your website. But in the end the more content you write, the more you can easily be found.

Traffic with Ads

Another piece of the puzzle to being found online is with paid traffic. You design an ad that you can advertise on Facebook, Google, LinkedIn or anywhere your target market hangs out online. They will click on your ad and head to your website.

You can combine both for a stable long-term strategy. Organic traffic is useful because when you are listed with search engines, traffic keeps coming in. It's out there; it is set. But do not rest too much on your laurels as your competition is getting smarter too.

Paid traffic allows you to have eyeballs right away, but when you stop advertising, no more traffic is coming to your website.

Nowadays, paid ads have come a long way. With customers sharing their preference, this data is used to tailor advertising.

This makes it easy for your ad to appear only to the ones who are looking for it or have mentioned on their social profiles that they have an interest in it.

WordPress

One of the best platforms to design websites that I recommend for business owners is WordPress.

WordPress makes it easy to have a footprint online; you can easily update it, it is easy to manage, and easy to scale with different plugins. Also, later on, if you need extra features and customization, you can hire a developer. They are readily available.

With WordPress, you have an array of templates available, some free, some paid. It is convenient and straightforward to design your website or blog.

Once you have a website, make sure that it is optimized. WordPress makes it easy here as well. You could get a plugin such as Yoast SEO. There is a free version and a paid version, any of those will be a great way to start optimizing the different pages on your website.

Landing Page

I am often asked between a website and a landing page what is better? I would say a landing page: because a landing page allows you to get the information from your customer. As a business, the list of your customers is the most important thing that you'll ever have.

But a well-optimized website can drive traffic that you can capture with a landing page. As such, they work in synergy.

Social Media

Let's look at social media now as our next element for a great footprint online. With social media, though, you need to be careful and know what is the purpose of the social media platform that you're going to choose.

You have Facebook, Twitter, LinkedIn, YouTube, Snapchat, Instagram and many others. They all have different purposes. As an example, LinkedIn targets professionals, YouTube is all about videos. What is your strategy and what is your goal? I'm sure for a lot of businesses they still want to get customers out of it.

Social media's most significant advantage is creating a community of fans of your products. They can interact with you. You can join in their conversations and read about their feedback, good or bad. You can also keep them updated about your business.

Some business owners might be afraid of social media because some customers could talk negatively about their business. The thing is, they are already talking about it somewhere. It's definitely to your advantage to join their conversation and interact with them and see how you can help and maybe change their perception of your business.

You could also take the opportunity, now and then, to drive people to your exclusive landing page for a free report, free consultation or free gift.

Another use of social media will be sharing the content of your blog if you have one. People are going to start commenting on your blog posts and you can join in the conversation.

Keep in mind, with social media you're renting a space. You're just a tenant. The social media platform can at any point change their rules, and they often do. It could impact your business if all you were doing were relying on those social media pages.

Remember Myspace? With them disappearing, all your efforts disappear as well. Yesterday was Myspace, but tomorrow it could be Facebook.

3.4 MAKE USE OF GOOGLE MAPS

Nowadays customers go online to look for businesses, and if you're not on Google Map, you are making a huge mistake. You should be on Google Maps. It is easy to set up. Go to https://www.google.com/business. Drive your happy customers to leave reviews on Google Maps.

You have other review sites such as Yelp and Foursquare where people can leave reviews for your business. Some of those websites are more used than others, but the big Kahuna is Google Maps. Make sure you're on it. Send a thank you note to customers that leave you positive reviews. They will make note of it and will be more than willing to write another review or do you a favour in the future.

Take immediate action regarding any negative reviews. Understand what the customer wanted and what you can do to make it right.

With Google Maps, you have the opportunity of getting more social proof with reviews left on your profile. But you need to be cautious.

We don't usually catch reviews that hurt us over time. You have a customer that had a bad experience, you were not aware of it, and the customer went online and left a bad review that hurt you.

If you've been in business for a while, you know sometimes some things happen that are out of your control. You did everything that you could, but the customers still had a bad experience. But at the end of the day, it's not that bad experiences don't happen, but when it happened what did you do about it?

In any products or services that you make available to customers, have at least a way for them to contact you directly. You will be aware of problems that arise, and you can take the proper action in solving it. When you're able to go and solve the problem, you're coming in ahead. Your customers will have a better experience.

On one of your products, this could be implemented as such:

If you have a negative experience with our services call this special 800 number, you will get a call back guaranteed.

The customer knows that whatever happens, you have their back.

3.5 HUDDLE

If you're in any kind of business and have a team, take the time in the morning to set the tone for the day and have a quick huddle with your team.

The huddle could be on the phone or face to face. It could be 5 minutes, 10 minutes, or 15 minutes. No more than that because you need to open doors for business. You could discuss what happened the day before, get feedback from some of your employees, and give directives.

Some employees have great ideas, but nobody is taking the time to hear them. Nobody is giving them the opportunity to talk. If you solicit feedback from your employees, you are going to hear great ideas that you can implement in your business. Those ideas could skyrocket your business.

Also, whether your employees are in sales or marketing or not, they should join your huddle. The truth is everybody in your business is in sales and marketing. It does not matter if the employee is in the accounting department. Any employee who is in touch with a customer is in sales and marketing. But even if they have no customer touch, take the time to bring everybody together. That employee in the accounting department can be an evangelist of your business outside of work hours talking with friends and acquaintances.

As a small business, you might have a team of 5, 10 or 15 employees. It is doable. With 50+ employees it tends to be more difficult, but at that point, you would have key managers doing huddles with their team instead of you.

3.6 INCENTIVES FOR EMPLOYEES.

A great thing that you can do is having incentives for your employees when they generate a lead.

As an example, if you have an accountant that is bringing a lead, your incentive could be a gift card or a guaranteed lump sum that will be added to their paycheck for each referral.

Some employees will not act if there are no incentives, as they still feel that it is not their responsibility. But when you have an incentive, now it's a different story. They become engaged.

3.7 EDUCATE YOUR STAFF

Make sure you educate your staff. Add regular training at your company. I know it can be expensive. It takes time from the day to day activity that employees need to do, but it is really important to educate your staff.

Educate them not only on your products but also on your perfect customers. Review with them the message that you are trying to convey to your customers.

Does your staff know by heart the features and benefits of your products? Do you have any recent promotion that your customer should know?

Make sure your staff knows why people are coming to your store. The better your team knows, the better they can serve your customers.

3.8 DEVELOP AN ARRAY OF MEDIA FOR YOUR BUSINESS

Another strategy to implement in your business will be to develop an array of media about your business. Whether it is photos, videos, audios, reports, case studies, etc. you should create media that are going to show your expertise, let people know more about your business, and let them get to know you.

Something that is common online with a lot of businesses is when you find their company website, they often ask you to schedule a free consultation. Their websites will have a few words about their team, their services, and a few features of their services will be mentioned as well. That's what everyone is doing.

You will go a step further when you're able to show different photos. Photos of the practice, pictures of the staff, photos of happy clients and customers, photos of your products. People want to see that.

Videos go a long way too. I don't know if you are familiar with this: you hear a song on the radio. You don't like the song that much. The music video then comes out a couple of weeks later. Once you see the music video, it grabs you, and now you're in love with the song. That's the power of video. Whenever you can have a video about your business playing on your website or playing in your store or practice, it will have a significant impact on your customers.

Producing a video is also quite affordable nowadays compared to what it used to be 5 or 10 years ago. Just look at all the videos available on YouTube. A lot of people do those in their bedroom, and the quality is fairly good. If they can do that what is your excuse? Grab a Go Pro, or a Nikon D7100 or a Canon 80D and you are in business. You can also hire an intern or a college student.

Recording audio is relatively simple as well. You have a few solutions out there. Software such as Audacity (www.audacityteam.org) can be downloaded for free and help you record and edit your recording. If you are on Mac, don't look further than GarageBand which comes free on your Mac Computer. You will be able to produce audio in no time.

Any media that you have helps the customer get to know you; It's acting as a sales tool and a marketing tool when you are not there. Your customers can view, listen or read that media 24/7 either online, at their place of business or when they are home.

In this day and age, every business should be in the education business. It doesn't matter what business you are in. Whether you are a plumber, a dentist, a chiropractor, an accountant; set up an education system for your customers. Provide documentation about what you do. Customers will get it from you, or they will get it from somebody else.

It is best if they get it from you, you can provide a whole array of things that explain the reason you do what you do, what you're looking for in a customer, what is your process. Develop case studies and material that your target market will consume. They will love it, and you'll be able to keep them within your grasp.

3.9 MARKET YOUR BUSINESS WITH WORKSHOPS

Having a workshop is a tremendous added value to your business.

Educating your market and your community through workshops will allow you to be seen as an expert.

For a lead generation strategy, offer them for Free. You could also charge a small fee for it. The best way to know what works is to test.

The workshop could allow you to discuss a certain theme, issue or challenge that customers and clients have.

You can easily hold several workshops that cover a wide range of themes.

At the end of your workshop, a small advertising about your product and service is welcome. But keep the workshop focus on helping your attendees with the information they came to find. People will be turned off if all you offer is a sales pitch for your products.

Another benefit that your attendees will have from your workshop is it will allow them to network. Seeing other people that use your products and services will ease their mind because they will see they are not the only ones in that situation. They will also be able to share how they are using your products.

You are also able to shake hands and meet potential customers.

Interacting with them will enable you to keep a pulse on what opportunities lie in the market currently.

Focus on information and also on providing an excellent experience. Providing an excellent experience could mean having refreshments for your guest or make your workshop fun, relatable and entertaining. The more your workshop attendees like the experience of your workshop, the more they will be willing to do business with you in the future.

Very few businesses in your community are doing it; you will then set yourself apart in your community.

Also, make your workshop interactive as people learn best through doing instead of passively receiving the information.

You can hold a workshop at your place of business or find a local in your city if your place of business is not ideal for it. In case you need to find a meeting place in your city, check out co-working space. They are really flexible when it comes to renting their office or event room.

3.10 COMMUNITY EVENTS

A great marketing strategy for getting your word out is hosting a community event. At a community event, you could ask your customers to bring a friend, which would be a referral.

The type of events that I am referring to here are events where you are giving away ice cream to the community or maybe a small concert with a local rising star. People love that.

At the event, you take the contact information of your customers and their referral. You receive their name, email, address and/or phone number. At the very minimum, name and email address so you can follow up with them and start sending them a free report or your newsletter.

You will also take advantage of the occasion to ask your current happy customers for a testimonial or review. This can be recorded. The environment is different. It is not a business setting; the testimonial has another flair to it. Your customers will be relaxed, and they can give their testimonial in a pleasant mood.

Events also give you the opportunity to talk about them. Once you had a great event, you're able to share it in your newsletter. You're going to share videos, you're going to share pictures, and you can talk about it for a whole month. It gives you a lot of marketing material to talk about.

As you're sharing pictures, videos, and testimonials, customers who have missed the event will think they should have attended. The next time you will announce another event your attendance will grow.

You're having fun, and your customers are having fun. Other people see that you guys are having fun, and everybody is attracted to that. Your customers are going to talk about it. People like talking about unique things that other people do and trust me not a lot of other businesses in your market are doing it.

Also, you're not specifically required to hold the events yourself. You could be a sponsor to one of them. Some events have the Coke logo or Red Bull logo, these companies try to have their names everywhere. You might not be able to do it for the Super Bowl, but you could do it for an event that is happening in your neighborhood.

The event will have more weight in the eyes of your customer if it is community focused, meaning the main attraction is not your products or services. You will let your customer base know by email that you have sponsored a community event and you will be there shaking hands with people, maybe answering some questions. It will go a long way.

3.11 CUSTOMER THANK YOU EVENT

Have you been recently invited to a customer thank you event? Among the different businesses that you are a customer of, have you been called and told to attend a thank you event? No, probably not. If yes, how many times did it happen?

Nobody is really doing it in your industry. When you're able to do that, even if you just take one person and you say thank you to your customer, it goes a long way.

It creates publicity. It's good for marketing. You have a strong image in the community. It attracts business and customers.

3.12 HAVE CONTESTS

Earlier we discussed events, and workshops, now we will look at another great and powerful strategy: contest. Those contests are entertaining. They can occur at a frequency that you can specify. An example would be to have a contest every quarter, or every six months. It depends on you, but every quarter is good.

What you can do is throw a contest where you are asking your customers to send you the best caricature of them with your products as an example. Or maybe you are asking them to dress as a pirate. You will pick the 5 best customers out of it. People love this kind of stuff. People like to interact in this kind of fun way.

You're going to take those 5 customers to a free dinner. At the dinner, you take pictures; you interact with your customers, you learn about your customers, you learn how your product has impacted them, you learn about other opportunities where your product could fit well.

And what you do later on, and I hope you already know this, is send it as a newsletter to your whole customer list.

3.13 PRICE STRATEGY

A mistake that a lot of business owners make when it comes to their pricing is charging the same price for all their customers. You should at least have a base price and a premium price. You are leaving money on the table if you don't.

Some people are not concerned about price. They like luxury, prestige, and will want your "Mercedes package" or "Titanium Package." If you have a product or service, try to have different versions, and of course, the one that costs more is going to have a lot more value.

3.14 PLUGGING LEAKS

Earlier I showed you how to add new leads and get new customers, but it is expensive to do that. It's the most expensive way to go and get a customer.

One of your main tasks in refining your business will be to plug leaks in your marketing strategy. At the moment, if you don't have a follow-up sequence, if you don't have a newsletter, if you don't have a referral program or several referral programs, you're losing customers left and right.

You can get a customer for free through a referral. If you're able to implement some of the strategies mentioned in this book, you're going to have customers staying longer and spending more with you. And as you're adding new leads and new customers, your customer base will grow.

Let's continue learning about those golden strategies that will help you retain more customers.

3.15 MAILCHIMP

I would recommend for you to have an email automation service. The one that I usually recommend is MailChimp. It is easy to learn and start with. You have a free plan, and you could have a MailChimp plan with an autoresponder for about 10$ a month. It is affordable, and you have other plans as well depending on your needs.

MailChimp will get you started with sending follow up emails to your new leads; you could set up a newsletter with it and then stay in touch with your customer database. You can start with that and scale up later on and follow up with a letter, follow up with a postcard, follow up with a phone call if your budget and personnel available allows it. But to start an email follow up sequence with MailChimp will be a big step in the right direction if you do not already have that setup.

MailChimp allows you to see a few metrics. You can measure the effectiveness of your marketing and see what works. What gets measured and tracked, gets improved. You will see your open rates. You will see who is clicking and on what they are clicking. You're able to see all that.

I have used MailChimp for many years. Nowadays ActiveCampaign is working really well for me.

You can also have a look at other similar solutions such as Aweber or Constant Contact.

3.16 CUSTOMER RELATIONSHIP MANAGEMENT SOFTWARE (CRM)

I will also strongly recommend getting a CRM which is a customer relationship management software.

This is the software where all your customer data is stored. You can browse the information of a customer and view their history, what they have purchased, how long they've been with you, their address and a lot more information.

Some examples of CRM would be Salesforce, Zoho CRM, InfusionSoft, Hubspot CRM, FreshSales, and Ontraport. In your industry, there could also be a CRM that is more appropriate. I would recommend trying a few of them to see which one works best for you. They pretty much all offer trials. Some CRMs have an emphasis on certain functions and businesses. At the end of the day, personal preference plays a lot into which one you choose.

3.17 FOLLOW UP SEQUENCE

A follow-up sequence allows you to get repeat business, earn referral business, and increase the transaction size of your customers. If you do not have one implemented, you are leaving significant money on the table.

Here is a quick story. I went to Cancun in the Quintana Roo area in Mexico recently to do some diving there. I went to a dive shop to get some pricing, and they got my information. They sent me one email, and that was it. I never heard back from them again. I am pretty sure that they had some outings every day or on weekends. They knew that I came to get information, but nobody followed up with me to check if I was still in town and if I was still interested to come by because there were these activities that were happening.

It was easy, in my situation, to end up doing business with another shop and that dive shop would have lost a sale. A lot of businesses make this mistake and, in the process, leave money on the table.

Do not count on the goodwill of your customers, prospect or leads to come back in your place of business. Follow up, follow up, follow up with your leads to make sure that they become customers and once they become customers to make sure you still remind them that you exist.

3.18 PARTNERSHIPS

Partnerships can be extremely beneficial to your business. They are powerful in helping you gain new customers and adding additional revenues to your cash register.

The key to a partnership is approaching auxiliary businesses that do not compete with you. Always have a WIN-WIN-WIN approach, where all parties benefit. That is the only way for sustainability.

If you try to take advantage of people, you need to find new partnerships to set up again all the time. It takes a considerable amount of time that could have been put into your business. But before long, word will be around town that you are not trustworthy and a no-no to do business with.

For an example of a partnership see the following: if you're a dentist, you can approach a chiropractor. The dentist would contact the chiropractor and see if he can offer the chiropractor's customers his services. For any client that would come from that offer, the chiropractor would get a 25% kickback on the amount spent by the client. It is a new client for the dentist. The chiropractor gets additional revenue out of his current clients. The customer/client gets their needs taken care of. A WIN-WIN-WIN.

Another example of a partnership would be a web developer who reaches out to an SEO agency. The customer base is about the same: their customers want to have a presence online.

3.19 TRACKING

I mentioned earlier that you could track results with MailChimp. You can definitely do that with all the other media mentioned as well, whether it is a postcard, a letter or even a phone number.

With a toll-free number, you can have a number that is primarily dedicated to a unique marketing campaign. You're able to track how many phone calls are coming through. You can know how successful the campaign is.

With postcards and letters, you can have coupon codes or a special link. If you have a special link, a special website, a special URL that you offer the customer to go to with a coupon code attached to that, you can know how your marketing campaign is doing.

3.20 PAID ADVERTISING EFFECTIVENESS

It is best to focus on paid advertising because it is reliable. I don't know if you've already advertised on Craigslist. If you're in Canada, they use Kijiji more. You post an ad and before you know it your ad has been flagged and has been deleted. It could be the result of your competition not liking your ad. Craigslist has its place but it might not be ideal for good advertising.

With paid advertising, we know that we're paying for it and we know our ad is going to run.

Paid advertising allows us to know if our money is well spent. If it is working, how much are we getting back from it?

If we're spending 100 dollars how much are we getting back? Let's say we get 2,000 dollars back, the return on investment is 1900%.

If, on the other hand, we also do not get any customers to visit our place of business, we know that either the ad itself is flawed or the medium where we advertised is flawed.

We're able to know which ad is working and which ad is not

working and make proper adjustments.

3.21 HAVE FUN WITH YOUR MARKETING

If you're not having fun with your marketing, you're doing it wrong.

Marketing should be fun. It also should be the most important and crucial activity in your business. It allows you to be creative when showing what you are about, how you show yourself to the world, and what your products or services are.

Have fun and make your marketing exciting. If it's not appealing to you, it's not going to be exciting to strangers who come in touch with your business.

3.22 SMILE

Smiling is very simple. It's very small, but at the same time, it has an enormous impact. It is also easy to ignore.

Jim Rohn, who was hailed as one of the greatest business philosophers of our time, often said: "What is easy to do is also easy not to do." Smiling falls into this category.

There are a lot of businesses where you will go in, and nobody is smiling; nobody is welcoming you. Customers do not only want you to solve their problem. A lot of times they're looking for a place to belong, because we're social animals.

Sometimes, customers who feel that they have not been well received or that they do not belong will stop doing business with you without you realizing it.

A Chinese quote says, "a man without a smiling face, must never open a shop." This just tells you that smiling for your customers and smiling when you do business is a must.

3.23 YOUR MARKETING SCHEDULE

Marketing should be the main priority in your business. Marketing and sales are the pillars of business and drive everything. Nothing really happens before one of your products is sold. Marketing and sales help to reach that objective.

Make time each week for marketing. Sometimes, it's tough for small business owners to do so. But make it a priority and set it up on your agenda.

You can start with an hour a week for marketing, and later on, you could increase it. Review the activities that have been done, what revenue has been generated, what needs to be done next.

Schedule your marketing on your agenda, and you will have greater control over how your business grows. Just do it. Don't be a victim.

3.24 BUSINESS IS A COLLECTION OF CUSTOMERS

A business is a collection of customers.

Take this as an example. Let's say you have a shop today. You have been in business for several years. Your shop burned down but you still have a list of your customers. You open a new shop in another neighborhood a month later. You send some information through a newsletter, a letter or an email to your customer list letting them know what happened: that you had a fire and you are at a new location. People are going to come and do business with you.

Compare it to somebody that buys a business, but they had no customer information. Or they did not retain that information, or you're a new business. Nothing will happen, you have to start all from scratch. The shop that burned down would get customers there faster than the brand-new business.

Business is a collection of customers and making sure that you get customers, but also retain the ones that you already have, is one of your main priority.

3.25 GETTING A NEW CUSTOMER IS LIKE DATING

A great analogy that I can give you about business and customer attraction is getting a new customer is a lot like dating. It is like getting into a new relationship. Just like in dating, the customer needs to feel comfortable every step of the way.

You should have different offers, different price points to ease customers to get to know you. If you are a man, you don't walk up to an unknown woman today and ask her to marry you. She doesn't know you; she doesn't know what you're about. After a bit of small talk and banter, you would get her number and plan for the first date.

When you advertise, you don't ask customer right away to buy a 5-thousand-dollar product; you need to ease them along. Develop a free report, have a product option for them that they can try out at around $60, then have another option for them at 500$+ and more.

Dentists will have teeth cleaning and exam either free or at a very attractive price. Once the patient is in their dental practice chair, they will offer other services: straightening teeth, whitening teeth. Those services cost a lot more compared to teeth cleaning.

3.26 TESTIMONIALS

One great thing you can do with testimonials is to have them in several different formats.

You should have some testimonials in a text format, some testimonials in audio, and some testimonials in a video format. They are all powerful.

People respond in different ways. When you have your testimonials available in various formats that people can easily relate to and understand, you definitely put yourself in a better position.

3.27 ANSWER CALLS PROMPTLY

If you are a shop, store or business where people make inquiries by phone, make sure that those calls are answered promptly. This is often neglected.

If you can, you should answer calls at the first ring. What it shows to the customer is you want the business. You are ready to serve.

Have the person on the phone speaks loud and clear. You'll be surprised a lot of times with some businesses you can't perceive or understand what they are saying.

The person answering the phone is the first point of contact for your business. Like it or not that interaction will weigh heavily on what would-be customers think of your company.

You could also from time to time make sure that everything is being done as you instructed and is going smoothly. Call your store anonymously. One of the greatest entrepreneurs that I studied, Sir Richard Branson, used to do just that. He would pass as a customer and call to make an appointment to see how the flow was going.

You might find things that you had implemented, that no longer work. You will also be able to judge if the person responding to those calls is doing it well, and you can train that person and make the appropriate changes.

3.28 REFERRALS

Big companies take full advantage of referrals. So should you.

This is the case with Facebook.

When you sign up for Facebook, they ask you at the very beginning to send an email to your friend list, or import your email list, or connect your inbox for them to get the different emails that you have there.

Once they have a list from you, they email your friends letting them know: "Your friend, John, is on Facebook, you should be here too" which is powerful.

Using this strategy, a lot of software companies grew fast. It was free for them to import your friend list and send an email. They didn't have to have a poster, make a commercial, advertise during the Super Bowl. No need for a Billboard, no need to be on the radio. It was basically free, and they took advantage of it.

Referral is a robust strategy to implement in your business. If you do not have a referral strategy or even better 2 or 3 strategies to acquire referrals, you are turning your back on free customers.

3.29 CONTINUOUS LEARNING

You should keep on learning about marketing. Things change all the time; new technologies arrive on the block all the time, new marketing tools become available to you.

You need to sharpen your axe. It will allow you to refine the strategies that you have implemented. You will be able to see new "tricks" that would work well for your business. And it is a great thing because you can learn from other people's mistake, you don't have to make those mistakes yourself.

4 OUTRO

We covered a lot of ground. We talked about the different ways to attract customers, but we also went deeper and saw what are the few other things that you should do in your business to put more dinero in your pocket.

Let's recap what we learned.
- You can attract new leads using a lead generation system with a free report and a landing page.
- We identified your target market.
- We looked at how to drill into your customers' challenges, and how to differentiate yourself.
- We saw what media to use for an effective marketing system that will allow you to track your return on investment. Those media are flexible in the amount of money you could spend.

- We explored ways your customers could easily try your product.
- We went through 25+ strategies that would allow you to retain and nurture leads, and to increase your revenue.
- And much more…

It is easy to feel overwhelmed, but don't be. The best advice I can give you is to set aside time and implement the marketing strategies step-by-step. The best way to eat an elephant is one bite at a time.

Make sure you take action on what you have discovered throughout these chapters.

For some, this eBook will be plenty to get started. But others might require a little more handholding. Just like learning how to drive, after reading the driving code (this eBook), you would drive around town with someone more experienced on your side. For those who want to have their hands held through the process, I am available for consulting.

I offer a free strategy session.

To learn more visit: https://www.provenmarketingmachine.com/free-strategy-session/ or send me an email at consulting@provenmarketingmachine.com

Remember for these strategies to work, they need to be implemented, tested, and adapted to your business.

I am confident that if you take the time to put in place 3-5 strategies, you will increase the number of people who want to do business with you, retain more customers, and put more money in your pocket.

Don't be a tourist. Don't be a victim. Get to work.

To stay in touch with me and receive fresh marketing tips and strategies, you can subscribe to my newsletter https://www.provenmarketingmachine.com/newsletter/

You can also download a free report that I've made available for you: "The 5 Deadly Mistakes Small Business Owners Make". You can download it at https://www.provenmarketingmachine.com/report-deadly-mistakes-business/

If you have benefited from this book in any way and would like to leave a review on Amazon, it would be greatly appreciated.

For any questions or comments, please feel free to email us at info@provenmarketingmachine.com

With that said, get into HUSTLE MODE.

Godspeed.

Krishna

ABOUT THE AUTHOR

Krishna Diamesso is an author, traveler, entrepreneur, consultant, and marketing specialist. He likes to call the world his home as he has lived in 20+ cities across 5 continents. To discover more of his work, please visit his website at https:// www.provenmarketingmachine.com/

www.ingramcontent.com/pod-product-compliance
Lightning Source LLC
Chambersburg PA
CBHW072203170526
45158CB00004BB/1747